# IN THE REALM OF PROPHETIC DREAMS

WOODROW POLSTON

Woodrow Polston

# IN THE REALM OF PROPHETIC DREAMS

WOODROW POLSTON

Woodrow Polston

In the Realm of Prophetic Dreams
---

Copyright by Woodrow Polston 2018

All Scripture quotation from King James Bible, NIV.

Published by Polston House Publishing LLC. Printed in The United States of America.

Cover design by Polston House Publishing LLC. Artwork used from the public domain.

Polstonhouse.com

In The Realm Of Prophetic Dreams

# CONTENTS

Introduction............................................................7

1 God's Theater....................................9

    Dreams in the Bible..................................
    Revelation of Divine Purpose..............
    Warnings and Woes....................................

2 Terrors of the Night..........................21

    Nightmares from the Enemy................
    Recurring Dreams..................................

3 Visions of Judgment.........................29

    Asteroids and Earthquakes...................
    Chaos in the Cities..................................
    A Famine in the Land............................

4 A Hope of Things to Come................41

    Walking in Your Promised Land...........
    Wandering in the Wilderness...............

5 Dream Sharing................................47

    Did we Just Have the Same Dream?.....
    Others Around the World.....................

| | | |
|---|---|---|
| 6 | Witness to the Apocalypse……………….55 | |
| | When Angels Attack…………………..….. | |
| | Suffering the Third Horseman……….…... | |
| 7 | Purpose of Dreams……………….…....…..61 | |
| | For Fellow Man……………………….…..... | |
| | For the Glory of God……………….………. | |

Notes………………………………….…..…...69

About the Author…………………………….…..71

Writing this Book……………………….…...…73

Dream References……………………….....……75

## INTRODUCTION

IN THE QUIET of the night. During the time of rest, from the grueling duties of day to day life, we sometimes slip into the dream world. Some of us more often than others. What is there, in that place? A glimpse into our future? Memories of exploits past? Or random images and thoughts that have played out in our sleep? Perhaps, all of the above.

Or could it be that our dreams hold something more? Could it be that the Lord God, Himself, is whispering into our sleeping conscious. Is He speaking while we sleep, entering into our minds when we cannot shut Him out with our daily distractions? What are the purposes of our dreams, will they ever be realized? Are the keys to unlocking our destiny within this dreamworld? I would like to think so.

Having had many recurring dreams of a blessed future that lies in store, I have also had dreams of war, famine and other woes to come. While confusing, I have realized it is possible however for God's people to be exceedingly blessed in the midst of chaos. We need only consider the exodus for this point. While the Egyptians were mourning the death of their first born sons, after all the terrible effects of the plagues, the Hebrews were walking away from their bondage with parting gifts! And though they were led through a barren wilderness, God provided their food and water. Every need was met for a remarkable forty year period!

Are there others that dream often? Are their dreams akin to our own? After all, if God is imparting knowledge of events that shall come to pass, those whom He is speaking to should be fixed in agreement. Let us take a look at some of the instances in the Bible where dreams have played a major role in the lives of the dreamers. From this we may discern which of our dreams be from God. What He is saying to us through them, and what their ultimate purposes are for our lives.

*"In a dream, in a vision of the night, when deep sleep falleth upon men, in slumberings upon the bed; Then he openeth the ears of men, and sealeth their instruction." Job 33:15-16*

# 1
# GOD'S THEATER

here are many instances in the Bible, that depict the dreamworld as a place of visions, which provide a means of communication. Wars, famines, disasters and the rise and fall of kingdoms are among some of the wonders that have changed the course of history. All such things have been seen and recorded aforetime. The hidden knowledge of which can often be the attribute of having had a dream. Let us consider the nature of a few prophetic dreams as revealed in the Bible.

*"And he said, Hear now my words: If there be a prophet among you, I the LORD will make myself known unto him in a vision, and will speak unto him in a dream."* Numbers 12:6

*"And it shall come to pass afterward, that I will pour out my spirit upon all flesh; and your sons and your*

*daughters shall prophesy, your old men shall dream dreams, your young men shall see visions." Joel 2:28*

*"But there is a God in heaven that revealeth secrets, and maketh known to the king Nebuchadnezzar what shall be in the latter days. Thy dream, and the visions of thy head upon thy bed, are these." Daniel 2:28*

From only a few verses, we openly see that God is a giver of dreams. Though we are available dreamers, a word of caution. Not all dreams come from God. Some dreams come from the enemy, some are the effects of daily nonsensical activity. Some are plain visions that require limited, to no interpretation. All of which we shall cover in detail later on. Let us consider the following accounts from the scriptures.

## *Dreams in the Bible*

Plausibly one of the most well known dreams of the Bible, was given to Joseph, in the book of Genesis. It was a symbolic vision of his destiny. He knew that it meant something, he knew that is was more than just a dream. He was excited and encouraged by it. He couldn't help but share it with his family. He was shown the sun, moon and stars bowing down before him. It was interpreted that these were symbolic of his father, mother and brothers. Surely he was emotionally overcome with such a vision.

## In The Realm Of Prophetic Dreams

He had to have an unction that his destiny was of major importance. Knowing this had to be very humbling. I believe that he was a very caring young man who was excited about a future in which he could bless his entire family, as his dream would suggest. His dream was not well received by his siblings however. It was the jealousy of his destiny that angered them. When they learned of his prophetic dream, they began to plot against him.

They must have known that it was more than a regular dream as well. If it were just an ordinary dream they would have laughed it all off. But they knew that he had something in store which they did not. I have wondered what would have become of his prophetic dream had he not told a soul. His brothers would not have been moved with anger, and he would not have been sold into slavery. Thus he would not have been in a position to see his destiny unfold.

For as a result of being sold into slavery, he was taken down a path that would lead to greatness. Where he would appropriate the highest position in all the land of Egypt, second only to Pharaoh. Not only did Joseph become a man who could save his own people in a time of famine, but also all the people in Egypt! What a destiny for a man to embrace! His story paints a kind of foreshadow of the coming Messiah Jesus. He came to save his people and they rejected Him. In the end, He would save both His people, the Jews and the gentiles!

Elsewhere in the Bible, God has not only given prophetic visions of one's future, but asked of them what they would desire!

> "*In Gibeon the LORD appeared to Solomon in a dream by night: and God said, Ask what I shall give thee.*" 1 Kings 3:5

Concerning prophetic insight of future world empires, and to what end they would come, the following was a King's dream.

> "*In the second year of his reign, Nebuchadnezzar had dreams; his mind was troubled and he could not sleep.*" Daniel 2:1

This dream, given to a prophet, is an amazing revelation of Jesus Christ.

> "*I saw in the night visions, and, behold, one like the Son of man came with the clouds of heaven, and came to the Ancient of days, and they brought him near before him. And there was given him dominion, and glory, and a kingdom, that all people, nations, and languages, should serve him: his dominion is an everlasting dominion, which shall not pass away, and his kingdom that which shall not be destroyed.*" Daniel 7:13-14

## *Revelation of Divine Purpose*

When God gives us dreams, I believe He is doing so for multiple reasons. Foremost, He is giving us a most powerful encouragement. If we have received a dream that depicts a victorious outcome for our life and ministry, then our trials and tribulations should pale in comparison. Also, when we receive an evil report, or any such false prophecy from the enemy, we have our dream to stand behind. Then can we boldly proclaim the fact that the devil is a liar!

Other reasons include divine instruction. Joseph knew that Pharaoh's dream depicted a famine. He had the knowledge to give Pharaoh the appropriate instructions.

*"It is just as I said to Pharaoh: God has shown Pharaoh what he is about to do.*
*Seven years of great abundance are coming throughout the land of Egypt, but seven years of famine will follow them. Then all the abundance in Egypt will be forgotten, and the famine will ravage the land. The abundance in the land will not be remembered, because the famine that follows it will be so severe. The reason the dream was given to Pharaoh in two forms is that the matter has been firmly decided by God, and God will do it soon. "And now let Pharaoh look for a discerning and wise man and put him in charge of the land of Egypt." Genesis 41:28-33*

Encouragement, instruction, and here is the big one. Faith! There is nothing like receiving a word, vision or dream from the Lord! When God is directly speaking to you personally it builds your faith. Whether it be through words or dream visions, it will always boost your faith in Him. Once you have heard from the Lord in such a manner, you will greatly desire and look forward to His next utterance.

Following are several keys that can be used in discerning between dreams from God, the enemy, or simple everyday random dreams. As I and my wife have had our share of dreams from God, we have also had a plenteous amount from the enemy. Here is what we best perceive to be true.

1. A dream that is from God will always be according to His written word in the Bible. You will never receive information or instruction that would contradict His nature. For example:

Let's imagine that you have a dream, or dreams that you are getting divorced. Considering that this dream involves your marriage, which is a covenant between you, your partner and God, it is important. I would immediately rule out this as a random dream. It is from God, or the enemy. Next, you need to discern what the dream is suggesting. Is it painting an enticing picture of the divorce?

If so, that would likely be the work of the enemy. The only instance I can imagine God giving a dream concerning divorce, would be if he were warning you that it was coming. In which case, you could put forth the necessary effort to save and repair your marriage. This evaluation would be according to God's written word: *"For the LORD, the God of Israel, saith that he hateth putting away"* Malachi 2:16

2. A dream that is from God will be prosperous to your spirit. It may include instructions, visions of troubled

times, but it will have an encouragement attached. For example:

When Joseph had interpreted Pharaoh's dreams, one could have claimed that they were visions of doom. They involved poor crops, sickly animals and ultimately a severe famine. But this was not a prophecy from the enemy. It was a warning from the Lord. A divine enlightenment for one to take action. Sometimes people, even the people of God, miss out on divine instruction. This is due to some being offended by direct instruction, which may require a correction of their perception or actions etc. Some are offended and do not receive, at the fault of the messenger.

Occasionally, a messenger from God in the form of a prophet or fellow Christian will deliver vital information in an undesirable fashion. They may come across as being judgmental. Or perhaps it concerns something that you do not believe to be any of their business. Perhaps they came across as being rude.

I have had instances in my life, where a messenger very harshly gave me instruction, in a very judgmental fashion. I thanked them for the instruction and walked away peacefully. Without even disagreeing with them. I experienced mixed feelings for a short time, but I heeded the instruction knowing this: Sometimes the messengers are a mess, but the message is still true.

## *Warnings and Woes*

When God gives us warning dreams, they serve two main purposes. One is to give us the opportunity to take preventative measures against a future event. Two, would be to prepare us for something that will inevitably happen. This could be in terms of becoming mentally, physically, financially or spiritually prepared. Possibly all of the above. Some warnings may seem relatively insignificant, some may be a matter of life and death!

Let's consider some of the warning dreams that can be found in the Bible. First, God warns Abimelech, King of Gerar:

*"But God came to Abimelech in a dream by night, and said to him, Behold, thou art but a dead man, for the woman which thou hast taken; for she is a man's wife. But Abimelech had not come near her: and he said, Lord, wilt thou slay also a righteous nation? Said he not unto me, She is my sister? and she, even she herself said, He is my brother: in the integrity of my heart and innocency of my hands have I done this. And God said unto him in a dream, Yea, I know that thou didst this in the integrity of thy heart; for I also withheld thee from sinning against me: therefore suffered I thee not to touch her. Now therefore restore the man his wife; for he is a prophet, and he shall pray for thee, and thou shalt live: and if thou restore her not, know thou that thou shalt surely die, thou, and all that are thine."*
Genesis 20:3-7

In this account, God has seen the intentions of a king toward the wife of His prophet. Knowing that the king was about to make a grave mistake, He warned him to abandon his desires. This was a warning that demanded immediate action. Let us consider another dream that would demand an urgent response.

*"And when they were departed, behold, the angel of the Lord appeareth to Joseph in a dream, saying, Arise, and take the young child and his mother, and flee into Egypt, and be thou there until I bring thee word: for Herod will seek the young child to destroy him."*
Matthew 2:13

Here, God has sent a warning that required a move of location. Consider the comparison between the two dreams.

1. God is protecting His people.

In these accounts, God is helping His people, who happen to be very important according to His plan. If you have received a dream from the Lord, count it as joy! This is proof that you are an important part of His plan.

2. God will give a dream to others for your sake.

When God gave the warning dream to King Abimelech, it was to save his life. But ultimately, the dream was sent for the sake of His prophet, Abraham.

We have to wonder why God didn't give Abraham a warning dream, instructing him to admit that Sarah was his wife. Perhaps that would not have yielded the best result. This tells us that God will not only give us dreams for our benefit, but He will give dreams to others for our sake as well.

It may require trial and error the first time you receive a warning dream. One of the worst feelings in the world is writing off a warning dream. There have been a few instances where I had to go through situations that were nearly unbearable. Those uncomfortable life circumstances that make one question God. The heart breaker, is when He answers and says "I warned you but you didn't listen."

Often times the best way to learn something, is to make mistakes. As you can imagine, I listen much more carefully now that I can better perceive God's instruction. Following are several more keys to recognizing God given dreams.

1. The dream will stand out.

When I have had a dream from the Lord, and my wife would agree, there is something notably different about it from other dreams. The dream will stand out, you won't easily forget it. It will not be vague or foggy in your memory. Some dreams that we have had are as perfectly clear now, as they were when we awoke from them, years ago!

2. There will be confirmation.

If you question whether or not a dream was from God, the best way to ask is through prayer. If you do not receive an answer right away, be watchful throughout the day. The confirmation may come through the words of a friend or family member. Perhaps the confirmation will be revealed in an article you read, or a television program. You may even receive the answer from a total stranger!

3. It will be for the benefit of the Kingdom.

If your dream does not profit yourself, others, or the kingdom of God then it is not from God. If your dream projects your own profit and prosperity alone, for selfish ambitions, it is not from God. Remember the dream that was given to Joseph, how his family had bowed down before him. It was realized that he was most worthy, for his selfless ambition to help others.

## 2
# TERRORS OF THE NIGHT

hen considering the efforts of the enemy against our lives, the dreamworld is no place of sanctuary. In fact, the Devil quite often works effectively there. Sometimes, he will even twist and distort a dream previously received from God. Looking back at the various dreams that I have experienced, I would estimate that I have had many more dreams from the enemy than from God. As is the likely case with many Christ followers, the enemy has come strongly against my life.

When I had begun to write this book, I simply finished the outline before going to bed. As I slept, I received a vicious dream from the enemy. It was very discouraging. In fact, it stopped me dead in my tracks. And more than two years went by before I began to work on it again. It was the kind of dream that causes you to gasp as you awake. The kind that you don't soon forget.

It should have been evident what was happening to me. I was beginning a new work for the Lord and the enemy was attempting to shut it down. Now and then I suppose we lose some of the battles. But we know that the war is ultimately won by the Lord.

## *Nightmares From the Enemy*

"Nightmares are lengthy, elaborate dreams with imagery that evokes fear, anxiety, or sadness. The dreamer may wake up to avoid the perceived danger. Nightmares can be remembered upon awakening and may lead to difficulties returning to sleep or even cause daytime distress.

"Isolated nightmares are normal, but when dreams that bring extreme terror or anxiety recur often they can become a debilitating sleep disorder. Occurring during rapid eye movement (REM) sleep, a nightmare is a dream that results in feelings of extreme fear, horror, distress, or anxiety. This phenomenon tends to occur in the latter part of the night and often awakens the sleeper, who is likely to recall the content of the dream." - *Psychology Today* [1]

Having a bad dream is not an uncommon thing. Many of us have had our share of nightmares, I'm sure. But to what or whom is the blame? Some who study in professional fields, would suggest that having a nightmare could be the result of your diet. Or the temperature of your bedroom. Possibly stressful events of daily life. Maybe all of the above?

In The Realm Of Prophetic Dreams

If you want to believe that a pizza or late night burger caused you terror in the night, go right ahead. But I know this, that there is an adversary roaming about, seeking whom he may devour. Who also is called the prince of the power of the air. I know from experience that late night pizzas, burgers, potato chips and any number of different junk foods are not the cause. I have eaten all of the above without having a nightmare as a result.

There are some dreams that seem to be nightmarish in nature, but are not necessarily from the enemy. One such dream that I had years ago, was a vision of unfortunate circumstances to come. In the dream, I was standing outside of a small home on a country road. It seemed to be surrounded by flat fields of farmland. There were a few mature trees just down the road from the house. The scenery reminded me of some old painting of a rural landscape.

As I was standing in the small yard between the house and the road, I took notice of the dark clouds in the distance. As I looked around, there were large tornadoes forming in every direction. They seemed to be about a mile out, and were closing in. There was nowhere to run. The wind was picking up. All I could do was stand there in hopelessness.

After waking from the dream it was evident that it was of some significance. The conclusion that I came to was this, that it represented severe trials that were coming my way. I would have to go through them, and there would be no chance of escape. Unfortunately, these trials lasted for several years.

## *Recurring Dreams*

When you repeatedly have the same dream, over and over again, there is something to it. In my experience, my wife and I have both had multiple different recurring dreams. Some of which we have actually shared! Which we will cover later. The first recurring dream that I experienced and perhaps the longest running, is a dream where I am hunting. Most commonly with a bow, but occasionally with a rifle.

## In The Realm Of Prophetic Dreams

In the dream, the animal, sometimes a deer, sometimes a mountain lion, will come into shooting range. I draw the bow and shoot the arrow. Or I fire the rifle, depending upon the dream. After successfully hitting the target, I begin to track and retrieve the animal. When I catch up to it, I realize that it is no longer a deer, or mountain lion, but rather it is a human being. In most of the dreams, the person is severely wounded. In a few of the dreams however, they were fatally wounded.

After awaking from these dreams, which are ultra surreal, I have a terrible, regretful sensation. Much like I wold imagine someone would feel after accidentally killing someone. What a horrible feeling! Before the dream ends, I stand before the wounded victim knowing that they will likely die before help can arrive. I would estimate that I have had this dream in various forms, more than twenty times over the course of about five years.

I have to ask the classic question regarding these dreams. Are they from God or the enemy? I suppose that I have theorized both possibilities. If the dreams were from the enemy, the motive could simply be to deter me from doing what I enjoy during the Fall and Winter months. I often go fishing also, but enjoy it much less. I suppose that is why the dreams aren't involving a drowning right?

Most likely, the dreams are from God. I believe the purpose would possibly be to make me cautiously aware of my surroundings. I have always been an ethical hunter, and I have much respect for wildlife, nature and of course human life above all. So having had so many of these dreams, I had to take some means of action.

Aside from being extra attentive while in the woods, I have avoided hunting public land. Where my chances of encountering fellow hunters would dramatically increase. Thus, reducing the chances of being involved in an accident. While hunting has become a deep root in the genetic makeup of our household, Nothing is worth risking another person's life. So I challenge myself and my family to excel in safety awareness.

The second most common recurring dream began recently, after the death of my daughter. She had fallen sick as did we all in early March, from a common stomach virus. But we had all recovered as she still became sicker. Which was shocking to us, as she had been healthy her entire life. At the age of seventeen, she was admitted to the hospital, not realizing she would never come home again. We stayed by her side in the hospital, for the entire month before her demise. The entire stay was like a cruel nightmare. We could barely sleep on the couch that we shared with doctors and nurses coming and going at all hours. And then there were the sounds of the machines, all on top of the general worry and concerns for our daughter.

The worst part had to be the ups and downs. They would tell us that she was improving and could look forward to being discharged. And then she would take a turn for the worst. After all was said and done, we had her admitted to the hospital for stomach pains and fatigue. Less than five weeks later, she died from brain injury after having her colon removed.

Coming home was hard. We had been forced to leave a part of ourselves at the hospital. A very dear part of us, that we would never get back again. Everything had suddenly changed. And everything was a reminder of that. We no longer set a table for five, it was now only four. Her favorite song seemed to play more often on the radio.

People say that the hardest time for those who lose a loved one are the holidays. I say the hardest time is constant. Unless you block it out. You cannot do so during sleep however. And that is when the enemy comes in to attack. When we are seemingly helpless. I would dream that we were still in the hospital. And that there was yet hope for her recovery. I would dream that the five of us were walking through a park on a family outing. But she could not hear me when I would speak to her, nor was she able to perceive that we were there.

The worst of the recurring dreams were very brief. I would abruptly be woken up by a voice that simply said "Angela is dead!"

As you can imagine, it is nearly impossible to fall back asleep after such an experience. I had a dream that she was still alive, but our other children were dead. On another night, I dreamed that she was still alive, but that she had been kidnapped and we didn't know where she was. Or who had taken her. It was all the more proof though, that the enemy surely gets his digs in every chance that he can.

When we have the same recurring dream, or a dream concerning the exact same content, there is surely something behind it. In many cases, I'm convinced that it's actually someone rather than something. Whether that someone be God, Satan or a person in your life, you will have to discern for yourself.

What can you do when the enemy attacks you in such a way? I will reveal two things that have worked great for myself. When you have a nightmare that wakes you from your sleep, try the following:

1. Pray and seek God.

When I have suddenly awoke from a bad dream, the first thing I would do is pray. Seek God, praise Him and give Him glory. If the enemy is near, this will cause him to flee.

2. Recognize the attack for what it is.

If the enemy is attacking you so severely, there is a reason! He is aware that you belong to God, and he sees that God has great things in store for you. He will try to discourage and torment those who follow God at any cost. Thus, having come under attack is the evident sign that God is moving in our lives! As strange as it may sound, an attack is a reason to rejoice and be encouraged!

# 3
# VISIONS OF JUDGMENT

here are many examples in the Bible that depict terrible judgments to come. The book of Revelation is made almost entirely of this subject matter. Today, even outside of the scriptures, many people are receiving dreams and visions of things to soon come. After my wife and I were first saved, we devoted much time to prayer and fasting. We immediately began to experience dreams that were nothing like we had ever had. After researching information regarding some of the dreams, we realized that there were other Christ followers around the world dreaming very similar dreams.

Perhaps it was the fact that my wife had devoted a little more time to fasting and prayer than I did. But for whatever the reason, she seemed to have more frequent and vivid dreams than I. The dreams that I have experienced however, seem to be in agreement with those that she has dreamed. Following are several examples of dreams that my wife has had. Looking back at them now, certain things stand out to me, and only further confirm the legitimacy of the dreams. One such thing, is the fact that in her journal, she had noted that our oldest child was not present with us in the dream. This is significant in the fact that our oldest child has recently passed away.

The following dream was given to my wife in early 2012.

## *Asteroids and Earthquakes*

"The dream began with my family and I being away from home somewhere to the southeast of where we live. When there started to be earthquakes without ceasing we turned around and began to head home. We were east of the Mississippi river and we were having a difficult time finding our way back to the west side of the river. Many of the bridges were either out or blocked off. We finally found our way across the river and continued on our way home.

It was nighttime now and we stopped along the highway to get gas. My husband was pumping the gas when I looked at the sky and noticed an odd object there. The object appeared to be the moon, but it had a reddish sphere, like a soap bubble, around it. I told my husband that we needed to go now. As my husband hurried into our vehicle I watched the object in the sky. As I watched Something went through the air, almost as a shooting star but coming from the earth and going upwards. As it approached the object, the red sphere wavered and popped.

I quickly turned out onto the highway, when suddenly the sky lightened as if it was becoming daytime in the middle of the night. As we drove there was a sudden shock wave that hit us. I watched the trees to the side of the highway fold over toward the ground. Then the highway rippled and shook.

By now it was full daylight, but it was around two in the morning. As we continued to drive, slowly at this time because there were wrecked cars and parts of the road were broken, it began to snow. It was snowing, but it was not cold, this seemed to me that it could have been ash rather than snow.

The dream ended here.

Having moved forward from this dream I now see that this could be any number of events depicted in this dream. I also now believe that this was not the moon in my dream, but possibly an asteroid on a collision course with the earth. My husband also referenced this dream in his 2012 book, Preparing America For The Wrath Of God."

Another dream that she experienced a year later also depicts asteroids, or perhaps large hailstones falling from the sky.

"This dream came to me in the early morning October 25, 2013. I had awoke from my sleep and could not get back to sleep. I had been praying for some time when I was suddenly dreaming.

As the dream began, we are in a large SUV. My husband is driving, I am in the front passenger seat and our two youngest children are in the back seat, our oldest child is not with us. We are driving out of a good sized city when my husband suddenly makes and illegal u-turn. I asked him, "What are you doing?" He said, "I don't know." To which I was shocked and asked him, "What?!" He told me, "I am doing what the Lord told me to do!"

I didn't understand, but his answer was good enough for me so I sat back and was quiet. As we are driving I began looking at the sky. It was early morning and the sky had a predawn glow to it, but it was still dark and there were many visible stars. There was a fog-like haze in the middle of the sky. It was not low on the ground like fog nor was it high like clouds.

## In The Realm Of Prophetic Dreams

My husband said, "Look at the sky!" I noticed that I could see trails running through the haze, and I realized that it was raining rocks. I looked around and saw people starting to panic. Cars were wrecking and windows were being busted out of the city buildings.

We made the kids to get into the back of the vehicle because it had a large full-roof sun roof.

We opened the sun roof hoping that it would not break and shower the children with glass. Shortly after we realized that none of the rocks were hitting our vehicle at all.

As we drove further into the city we came to a large shopping area, which had streets that were closed to cars and only open to foot traffic. My husband stopped our SUV. The four of us looked at each other for a brief moment and then all got out without speaking a word. We came around to the front and all joined hands.

We walked into the area in front of us. People were running around and laying in the streets. Some of these people were terrified, some were injured and some were dead. As we walked further into this area we began to hear singing. We saw a park like courtyard area. There are benches, potted plants and in the center of the park area is a raised platform stage. The singing is getting louder. People are coming to this place singing a hymn of praise to God! We started singing too! As we sing we join the others singing and moving up onto this platform.

People around us are still going crazy and it is chaos around us. But those who know the Lord are untouched moving with one accord to this place. As we sing crowded shoulder to shoulder on the raised platform we lift our faces to the sky. It is still raining rocks, but they are hitting something invisible above us and bouncing away. We keep singing and looking upwards. Here the dream ended and I awoke."

Similar events are described in the book of Revelation. What is very comforting about this dream, and ultimately the message to take away, is that God protects His people. Even through the most terrible circumstances.

## *Chaos in the Cities*

In the event of a major natural disaster, war, or anything that would cause serious disruption of daily life, there will be great turmoil anticipated in the cities. A few years ago, I had a dream which involved such disturbing imagery. My wife and I were on a commercial plane, and it seemed as though we were flying out of the country from the mid-west.

## In The Realm Of Prophetic Dreams

During flight, something had gone very wrong on the ground. We were told that we wouldn't be able to leave the states. But for unknown reasons, we wouldn't be able to land at an airport either.

We began our descent over what I perceived to be New York City. We came lower and closer to the ground. There was a main broad way that was lined with sky high buildings. It seemed to go on as far as the eye could see.

As the wheels were touching down on the surface of the road, I was looking out the front window of the cockpit. There were burning cars here and there in the street. Bodies were littering the street and sidewalks. There was a mid size sedan burning in the street directly in front of us. There were several wounded firemen alongside the car. It seemed as though they were making an attempt to pull someone from the wreckage.

The plane violently bounced as we were landing, and shockingly we ran right over top of the firefighters, pushing the car aside. As we continue down this endless street, the scene remained the same. Fires, wreckage and bodies were everywhere. As the plane slowly came to a stop, we began to depart out of the main exit door. The people that were out walking on the street and sidewalks were crazed. Some were walking at a quickened pace, others were walking as if nothing had happened.

As we began down the sidewalk I heard gunshots. Even the sounds in this dream were surreal. It was not like the blast of a gunshot in a field or in the woods. Which carries it's voice for miles, to neighboring ears. Neither was it similar to the pulse of a gunshot inside of a house. Which sounds like a heavy book being slammed shut, or dropped onto a floor. But rather it was the boom of a raw explosion echoing between the buildings. Imaginatively comparable to hammering inside of a large concrete chamber.

Looking in the direction of the sound, I witnessed a man shoot another man as he walked along the sidewalk. It was a senseless murder, and I knew in the dream that he was killed simply because he was there. As we continue on, there were many other people shooting and murdering pedestrians as they were walking down the street. They were doing so just for the sake of killing. Their victims were nothing more than moving targets, in the wrong place at the wrong time.

After I awoke from the dream, I almost immediately thought of a verse from the book of Revelation. It was concerning one of the four horsemen.

*"And there went out another horse that was red: and power was given to him that sat thereon to take peace*

*from the earth, and that they should kill one another: and there was given unto him a great sword."* Revelation 6:4

In this dream, it was though a switch had been flipped in the minds of the people. Or as if they were obeying a voice in their head that seemed to simply say 'Kill'. I believe it was a vision of what that time will be like. There was no peace. Nothing would prevent such senseless violence.

## *A Famine in the Land*

In another one of my wife's dreams, we are living in a new house. she was also shown a large property that the house sat on. The property included crop fields as well as plenty of woodland. In her dream, she was shown strange aircraft that was flying over our property. It was not comparable to any aircraft that she had ever seen before. She did recognize however that it was being operated by the United States military. As she saw a passenger looking out of it who was wearing some type of U. S. military issue uniform.

After one of the aircraft landed nearby, our home was surrounded by military personnel, and they were pounding on the front door of our home. After opening the door, they came in and conducted a quick search. Afterwards, I accompanied them to another room where they spoke to me in private for several minutes. When we came out of the room, I showed them to the door and then they were gone.

After they left, she was sitting on our bed when I came to give her a strange message. I looked at her and said, watch out for the spiders. She then looked behind her, to see if there was a spider on the bed. She then asked, what spiders? Do you see a spider? Again, I said, watch out for the spiders! She replied, what spiders? When I answered for the last time, I said, beware of the black widows!

When she woke up, she shared the dream with me, and we began discussing a possible interpretation. There was no doubt that it was a warning dream, that regarded our future. One interesting detail of the dream, was that a glimpse of our children gave her the impression that they were about three to five years older. After reviewing the dream for less than five minutes, I determined three key words that we could use for a google search, in hopes of finding answers. The key words were, "military" and "black widows".

To our amazement, we immediately found answers to the strange dream that she had just experienced. The mysterious black aircraft that were in her dream, are also found in reality. The Black Widows, are a combat aviation company of the United States army. Based in Ohio, and Kentucky, They have a history that goes all the way back to world war 2. Their motto is 'mate and kill', and they are also known as 'the spiders'.

In a more recent dream involving this same property that has been the center of past dreams, we received far more revelation than any other before it. This dream not only served as a warning dream, but seemed to be an instructional dream as well. In this dream, my wife was lying in bed and looking at the moon through a skylight in the ceiling, when three angels came into view. Two of the angels were on each side of the moon, one was wearing a red robe, and the other was wearing a white robe.

The two angels seemed to take hold of the moon, and they pulled it back until it was no longer visible. It was then that the third angel came closer to the earth, until it was standing right before my wife. The third angel was wearing a blue robe, and we have interpreted that the revelation of this dream specifically effects the United States, because the angels were dressed in red, white, and blue.

She described a misty fog round about the angel, and it was then that she was shown crystal clear images. She saw vegetables and produce that were rotten, and she saw crops that were extremely undeveloped. After seeing these things, she was shown large groups of people who were fighting over food. And she was shown large cities that were filled with chaos, due to people rioting and widespread civil unrest.

After these visions, she was given a view of our own personal property. She saw a large garden that covered several acres, a large green house, and hundreds of acres of healthy crops. The most interesting vision in this dream, was a unique irrigation system that allowed us to have an abundance of crops to harvest, at a time when the majority of crop fields were failing. This unique irrigation system was shown to her in detail, and would no doubt pay off in the event of a severe drought.

When considering our prophetic dreams overall, there are two key points that are obvious in nearly each and every one of them. The first, is that perilous times are approaching, and that our nation is going to experience suffering of biblical proportions.

The second, is that we are going to be in a situation where we can help a lot of people. It goes without saying, that we will not be able to do such things without the help of God. So we have given our life over to the will of God, so that such things can be accomplished through us.

# 4
# A HOPE OF THINGS TO COME

hen the Hebrew people were brought out of Egypt, they were given a vision of the land which they would be taking. The description of it was amazing, a land flowing with milk and honey. The same promise is true today for those who become the people of God. Symbolically, we follow Him out of the world, 'Egypt', and He gives us new life.

Not only do we have eternal life to look forward to, but God gives to us a vision of a new life on earth as well. We should be looking for a kind of promised land as did the Hebrew people. Of course, that is assuming that we have given our life over to Him, and walked out of Egypt. Consider the following promise that was spoken by Jesus.

*"And Jesus answered and said, Verily I say unto you, There is no man that hath left house, or brethren, or sisters, or father, or mother, or wife, or children, or lands, for my sake, and the gospel's, But he shall receive an*

*hundredfold now in this time, houses, and brethren, and sisters, and mothers, and children, and lands, with persecutions; and in the world to come eternal life."* Mark 10:29-30

What an amazing promise! Have you given up your home for the sake of Jesus and the sake of the gospel? Perhaps a piece of land? Have you been separated from a close family member? If so, this encouraging word from the Lord, tells us that we will be most generously compensated both now in this life, and the life to come!

## *Walking in Your Promised Land*

In a world of trial and tribulation, it is very important to have a vision of hope. With that hope however, there must be faith. Even great faith I might add. What do you suppose kept Joseph going all that time? Having been in a pit, sold into slavery, and then thrown into prison! Imagine the struggle within his heart and mind. The dream vision of him being exalted, must have seemed like a lie from the enemy, completely contrary to reality.

But he kept on believing. Even when it completely defied logic. And that is where the faith comes in. For it is one thing to hope for something. But it takes faith to believe it will happen. And that faith is vital for enduring the struggles that lie ahead. I believe that when a prophecy is given to someone, the enemy does everything in his power to contradict it. If God has spoken a good word for your life, be on the lookout for the enemy. He will try to convince you that it was a lie.

You must also pray for that faith, that you yourself would be able to endure the time it takes to wait. Consider the following example that was spoken by Jesus.

*"The seed falling on rocky ground refers to someone who hears the word and at once receives it with joy. But since they have no root, they last only a short time. When trouble or persecution comes because of the word, they quickly fall away."* Matthew 13:20-21

There is likely no one in the world, who fails to receive good news with joy. There are multitudes however, who lack the patience to see it come to pass. Also, Jesus tells us in Matthew, that trouble or persecution comes because of the word. That is the enemy fighting the will of God for our lives.

After coming out of Egypt, there is a time of breaking down and rebuilding within ourselves, that we must endure. It involves a changing of the heart. A spiritual birth and awakening. Dying to one's flesh. A painful process that all must go through if they are to be refined.

## *Wandering in the Wilderness*

It has been my experience, that one of our greatest obstacles is the test of time. The passing of time alone, seems to be an indicator that our hope and vision has failed. Not only does the enemy work hard to convince us of this, but we ourselves are guilty also. We may begin to think that we have goofed up and ruined God's plan. Perhaps we tell ourselves that it was our imagination, or just a random dream or thought.

There is also the possibility that we have turned our back on God's plan. In which case the vision indeed would be canceled. Let us consider the characteristics of those who were unable to walk into their promised land.

1. Lack of trust in the Lord.

*"The Israelites said to them, "If only we had died by the LORD's hand in Egypt! There we sat around pots of meat and ate all the food we wanted, but you have brought us out into this desert to starve this entire assembly to death."* Exodus 16:3

Although they had been witness to the mighty signs and wonders of God, they continued to have doubt. This was an evident sign that they were resisting the spirit, and walking after the flesh. For it was the cause of their fleshly appetites and hungry bellies that they grumbled against God.

2. Willingness to return to Egypt.

*"That night all the members of the community raised their voices and wept aloud. All the Israelites grumbled against Moses and Aaron, and the whole assembly said to them, "If only we had died in Egypt! Or*

*in this wilderness! Why is the Lord bringing us to this land only to let us fall by the sword? Our wives and children will be taken as plunder. Wouldn't it be better for us to go back to Egypt?" And they said to each other, "We should choose a leader and go back to Egypt."* Numbers 14:1-4

Often, as believers, we do face opposition. We receive discouraging words, even from other believers. We are even tempted to turn back to the captivity of the enemy, and the bondage of sin. I know all too well from my own experiences. There is no road harder to travel, than the one that lies between Egypt and the promised land. But we have no choice except to keep going. Knowing that God is with us.

3. Constant complaints.

*"Now the people complained about their hardships in the hearing of the LORD, and when he heard them his anger was aroused. Then fire from the LORD burned among them and consumed some of the outskirts of the camp."* Numbers 11:1

Another trait that I confess to have shared with the Israelites. I have been in situations that I repeatedly complained about. All we can do sometimes is ask for forgiveness, learn from our mistakes and move on. Though it is much easier said than done. Consider Paul as our example, as he stated the following in his letter to the Philippians.

Woodrow Polston

*"I know what it is to be in need, and I know what it is to have plenty. I have learned the secret of being content in any and every situation, whether well fed or hungry, whether living in plenty or in want. I can do all this through Him who gives me strength."* Philippians 4:12-13

# 5
# DREAM SHARING

The ultimate purpose for sharing one's dream, is to seek out an interpretation, if there be one. Most commonly, dreamers will share only the dreams that seem to be of some unknown significance.

The sharing of dreams dates back at least as far as 3000 BC in permanent form on clay tablets. In ancient Egypt, dreams were among the items recorded in the form of hieroglyphics. In ancient Egyptian culture dream sharing had a religious context as priests were also known as dream interpreters.

Those whose dreams were especially vivid or significant were thought to be blessed and were given special status in these ancient societies. Likewise, people who were able to interpret dreams were thought to receive these gifts directly from the gods, and they enjoyed a special status in society as well.

The respect for dreams changed radically early in the 19th century, and dreams in that era were often dismissed as reactions to anxiety, outside noises or even bad food and indigestion. During this period of time, dreams were thought to have no meaning at all, and interest in dream interpretation all but evaporated. This all changed, however, with the arrival of Sigmund Freud later in the 19th century. Freud stunned the world of psychiatry by stressing the importance of dreams, and he revived the once dead art of dream interpretation.[2]

There have been several instances, that have shocked me concerning my own personal dreams. My wife would surely agree that she has been equally surprised. The most incredible instances involved us both having the exact same dreams!

## *Did We Just Have the Same Dream?*

While my wife and I have shared similar dreams, we have never before had the very same dream. We have both dreamed of a new house, but the details of the house were different. We have both dreamed of war and famine. Again, the details were similar yet different.

## In The Realm Of Prophetic Dreams

That all changed after a dream she had awoke from one morning.

She began to describe the dream to me. We were in the home of a world leader, one of the most powerful men in the world. I was in a study, or office with this man. She was in the kitchen with his wife and their two daughters. As she was talking with this woman whom she knew the name of, their two daughters came in to join them.

After she awoke from the dream, she described it to me and told me the names of those who were in her dream. I was shocked by the implications of being in the home of such a powerful world leader! This was anything but a typical, normal dream.

Prior to this dream, we had no knowledge of this man's private life. We did not know the name of his wife. We did not even know if he had any children. As we began to research information on him, the dream was all but confirmed to be an authentic dream vision from the Lord.

Our research confirmed not only that he and his wife have two daughters, but that his wife's real name is the same as it was in her dream! These two facts alone were seemingly impossible to be mere coincidences.

Several weeks had passed by, then I had the same dream. I was in a large study room or office with this man. I was conscience of the fact that my wife was there also, but in another room. I was standing next to this man's desk and considered myself quite privileged to be there.

After a month or two had gone by, I had another dream that involved this man. This time we were in a conference room. We were about to have a meeting that included perhaps six to eight other men. We were all wearing suits. As in the other dream, I was conscience of who this man was and privileged to be in his company.

A year or so had passed when it happened again. This time, it was I that had the dream first. I was standing near a train, whether or not I was boarding I am not sure. I was standing next to a former President of the United States of America. At the time of this dream, he had only been out of office for a very short time. I had not voted for him, nor did I agree with his ideals or values. In short, I did not like him.

In this dream, I was speaking to him as though he were a personal friend. I was lifting him up. It seemed as though I was giving all the effort possible to be encouraging to him. After waking up from this dream, you can imagine my state of confusion. I never would have imagined myself saying such nice things to someone I so strongly disagreed with! But there I was in the dream, warming right up to him!

It was immediately evident that this was a dream from God. It displayed two important themes concerning my walk with the Lord. First, it was an example of how we are to treat people, even those whom we strongly disagree with. It was also a picture of how the Lord has changed me. Second, it was for the Kingdom, for the glory of the Lord. Sometimes we have to go places and meet with people that we typically would not.

I didn't mention the dream to Miryah (My Wife) But I briefly thought about the dream a little later in the day. That night I had no dream. The next morning, after doing some gardening, we went inside to take a break. After having sat down with a snack and drink, She said:

*"So I had an interesting dream last night."*

*I replied: "Oh, what was it?"*

*She told me the dream:*

*"We were in a large waiting room. It was an official building. There were people coming and going and they were all dressed in suits. A man opened a door and stepped out.*

*"He will see you now." The man said.*

*We entered the office to speak with the man who was seated behind his desk. It was ...."*

At this point in describing her dream to me, she told me the name of the man who was seated behind the desk. It was the same man from my dream the night before! A former President of the United States! I couldn't help but interrupt her:

*"You're kidding me right?!"* I said. But there was no way she could have been. She had no clue at that point that I had just dreamed about this man approximately 24 hours before. I asked her to please go on...

*"As we approached the man's desk, he was shuffling through a stack of paperwork. When we presented ourselves before him, I began to witness to him. As I testified to him, the witnessing was even aggressive as I said: Only Jesus can save you from going to hell!*

*While we were witnessing the truth to him, he continued to shuffle through his paperwork.*

*"Is that it? Are we finished here?" Asked the man."* And the dream ended there.

After she had finished telling me the dream, I described my dream from the night before to her. She was equally amazed at the fact that we had such similar dreams about the same man. And we had not recently discussed him, heard any news about him or even given him any thought for that matter. All of these circumstances formed the right catalyst for us to boldly agree; this was certainly a dream from the Lord God!

## *Others Around the World*

Having experienced dreams with such prophetic implications, we have sought out similar dream experiences from others abroad. With little surprise, we found that the dream visions concerning earthquakes, famines and major wars were quite common. We discovered that many of God's people have had dreams and visions of area specific earthquakes. Area specific wars and judgments that align perfectly with what we have been shown.

One such example, would be a man of God having had a vision of a terrible earthquake here in the Midwest. It was as though it were a judgment that would almost literally tear the country in two. Some have had visions of such a massive earthquake happening on the New Madrid fault line, that the gulf of Mexico actually opened up and connected to the Great Lakes!

There have been dreams and visions concerning many troubling things that are to come. Not only to a certain region or nation, but to the whole world. We know from reading the Holy Scriptures that these things shall surely come to pass. However, I suppose that it is the possibility of seeing them come to pass in our own lifetime, that truly astounds us.

Throughout the book of Revelation, there are many judgments that will come upon the world in the last days. Such judgments can also be found in the books of the Old Testament. The good news for us of course, is that we are the children of God! We have escaped the wrath that is to come upon those of the world!

This does not suggest that we will not endure trials and tribulations. We that are called according to the purposes of God have the enemy against us. We may have to endure hardships, even terrible circumstances. But God is with us, He will not forsake us! What I am trying to say is simply this; that whatever we face, we know where we stand in terms of eternity. For this life is but for a moment, and we will be with Him forever more.

Having said that, there has never been a more urgent time in history than right now, to make sure that you are right with God. I encourage everyone to seek Him, to know Him and to serve Him. And doing so will be the greatest thing you have ever done in your life time!

# 6

# *WITNESS TO THE APOCALYPSE*

T here can be little to no doubt that we are living in the end of time. And that we are fast approaching the end of the age. As the book of Revelation details, there will be many chaotic events that take place. Perhaps one of the most terrifying of all, includes the invasion of an Angelic army, come to execute the judgments of God! This is plainly described in the epistle of Jude:

*"And Enoch also, the seventh from Adam, prophesied of these, saying, Behold, the Lord cometh with ten thousands of his saints, To execute judgment upon all, and to convince all that are ungodly among them of all their ungodly deeds which they have ungodly committed,*

*and of all their hard speeches which ungodly sinners have spoken against him." Jude 1:14-15*

## *When Angels Attack*

      Several years ago, perhaps 2015 or 2016, our daughter experienced a very interesting yet frightful dream. When she had awoke from it, she described it to us in great detail. In this dream, our family was shopping at a store. Two of us were in the store, and the other two of us were waiting outside in the car. As she looked up at the sky, there was an opening like a door, in which giants began to come through. She described them as being comparable to giant men dressed in ancient battle array.

As they lighted upon the earth, people were running away, screaming in terror! The giants were wielding swords and chasing after some of the people. After the other two of us came out of the store, we fled the scene, in an attempt to reach a remote location. In this dream, she was very afraid, as the manlike giants seemed to be chasing after us also.

When she described the details of this dream to us, it was immediately evident to me, that it could be a prophetic vision of a possible future judgment. It recalled the prophecy from the second chapter of the book of Joel:

*"Blow ye the trumpet in Zion, and sound an alarm in my holy mountain: let all the inhabitants of the land tremble: for the day of the Lord cometh, for it is nigh at hand;*
*2 "A day of darkness and of gloominess, a day of clouds and of thick darkness, as the morning spread upon the mountains: a great people and a strong; there hath not been ever the like, neither shall be any more after it, even to the years of many generations.*

*3 "A fire devoureth before them; and behind them a flame burneth: the land is as the garden of Eden before them, and behind them a desolate wilderness; yea, and nothing shall escape them.*

**4** *"The appearance of them is as the appearance of horses; and as horsemen, so shall they run.*

**5** *"Like the noise of chariots on the tops of mountains shall they leap, like the noise of a flame of fire that devoureth the stubble, as a strong people set in battle array.*

**6** *"Before their face the people shall be much pained: all faces shall gather blackness.*

**7** *"They shall run like mighty men; they shall climb the wall like men of war; and they shall march every one on his ways, and they shall not break their ranks:*

**8** *"Neither shall one thrust another; they shall walk every one in his path: and when they fall upon the sword, they shall not be wounded.*

**9** *"They shall run to and fro in the city; they shall run upon the wall, they shall climb up upon the houses; they shall enter in at the windows like a thief.*

**10** *"The earth shall quake before them; the heavens shall tremble: the sun and the moon shall be dark, and the stars shall withdraw their shining:*

**11** *"And the Lord shall utter his voice before his army: for his camp is very great: for he is strong that executeth his* *word: for the day of the Lord is great and very terrible; and who can abide it?"* - Joel 2: 1-11

What a fearful vision to behold! Yet another verse from scripture that came to mind was from the gospel of Luke:

*"Men's hearts failing them for fear, and for looking after those things which are coming on the earth: for the powers of heaven shall be shaken."* Luke 21:26

## *Suffering the Third Horseman*

In the time period of the tribulation, there will be death and destruction such as the world has never seen. Great wars that claim unimaginable numbers of lives. Hatred and murder, and criminal activity of epic proportions. The common theme among the diverse dreams we have experienced in our family, is one that mirrors such dreaded prophecy. Famine, wars, death, chaos and destruction.

Though there will be many woes to endure, there will still be hope for those who have not taken the mark of the beast. For those who place their trust in the Lord Jesus. Keeping in mind that this life is but a blip in time. A short lived, violent and intense experience for most. But we have in mind, that hope of a future in eternity, wherein there is no more pain, tears and suffering.

# 7
# Purpose of Dreams

There can be little doubt that there are important aspects to our dreams.. or at least some of them. While few dreams are obvious in both meaning and implication, others are more cryptic and require both prayer and study. All dreams that are God given have an important purpose. Let us consider what some of the reasons and purposes include.

Woodrow Polston

## *For Fellow Man*

Oftentimes when we receive a prophetic dream, we fail to initially look beyond the glory of it. If the dream vision reveals a breakthrough of some kind in your life, or an incredible promotion, it can be an amazing feeling. Especially when that dream vision is confirmed as a valid dream sent from God.

When we look beyond the initial shock and awe of the dream however, a clearer picture and purpose develops. When Joseph had awakened from the dream in which he was highly exalted *(the sun, moon and stars bowing down to him)* he must have felt like he was floating around on a cloud! But the dream did not reveal the true meaning or reason.

What the dream did not show, was the tribulation, torment and anguish that he would have to endure. I would imagine that after having been betrayed by his brothers, being sold into slavery, suffering imprisonment, he looked back at the dream and questioned whether or not it was all worth it?

The glory of exaltation and promotion comes with a price. In situations where God is going to use someone in such a mighty and important way, the tribulation is seemingly greater. I wonder if he looked back and thought it foolish or naive of himself to have expressed such excitement over his prophetic dream? Had he considered the tribulation he would soon face, I believe he would have likely put his face in his hands and spoke to no one of the dream.

Ultimately, the dream was lacking a revelation of why there was an exaltation to begin with. Typically, one is exalted for having accomplished a great feat of some sort. But in most cases, such accomplishments come only after there have been great and even terrible sacrifices on the part of the exalted. Similarly in modern culture, we often fail to see the poverty stricken humble beginnings of people who are extremely successful and wealthy.

The reason for his exaltation in the dream, was that he was placed in a position that would allow him to provide for many people, in a time of severe famine. The sun, moon and stars that were in his dream, were representations of his Father, Mother and his brothers. Whom did greatly benefit from his position of authority, along with many countless others who would depend on his provision.

If God has given you a dream that reveals a future promotion and prosperity, do everything you can to align your life with that dream. Keeping in mind, such dreams often take time, even many years to be fulfilled. Discouragement comes with waiting. But we must remember, there are many who are depending on us to keep the faith, and to see the dream come to pass!

## *For the Glory of God*

Above all else, God is glorified when prophetic dreams and visions come to pass. Above the dream, above the dreamer and above the situations involved. This one thing must needs be done. More important than having faith in it, believing it will happen, More important than aligning ourselves with the dream, is that we give God the glory!

When others whom you have told about the dream see it come to pass, this will also increase their faith in God. In so doing, they will be more likely to seek after Him, to desire to know His will for their life through dreams and visions.

As I look back on the dreams that I have received, they are numerous and astounding. But I must say, the most amazing thing about them, is simply that God would even take the time to communicate with me in such a way! He really is an awesome and powerful God. He has a plan, and little by little it is being revealed to those of us that are seeking after Him.

## In The Realm Of Prophetic Dreams

I anticipate that God is about to move in a mighty way, not only in the United States but in the world abroad. I believe that a 'latter rain' of Pentecost is very near. Many have been praying for it, and I believe that it may begin right here in the mid-west. Considering some of the dreams that we have experienced in our household, it certainly would not come as a surprise!

I believe that during this time, many signs and miracles will explode in the church. Many who are sick will be healed. Many who are lost will be saved. I suspect that the effects of this awakening will mirror that of the tent revivals of the early to mid 1900's. Bars and night clubs will shut down for lack of business. Crime will suddenly and dramatically drop. Everyone will be flocking to the church! What an amazing time it will be!!! And let the glory be to God for all that He is going to do!

Woodrow Polston

In The Realm Of Prophetic Dreams

THE END

Woodrow Polston

## NOTES

Interior art work from public domain.

http://etc.usf.edu/clipart/62600/62694/62694_church.htm

1. https://www.psychologytoday.com/conditions/nightmares

2. https://en.wikipedia.org/wiki/Dream_sharing

3. Angel Michael painting from public domain.

4. Four horsemen painting by Viktor Vasnetsov. From the public domain.

5. references   http://www.learnthebible.org

Woodrow Polston

## About the Author

Woodrow Polston is the Author of numerous books that are attributed to biblical studies. The President of Polston House Publishing, Woodrow is a licensed Minister who resides in Rural Missouri with his Wife and children. To learn more, or to book the Author for a speaking event, visit the website at Polstonhouse.com today!

Woodrow Polston

# Writing This Book

Though it is the shortest work that I have done in length, this book has taken several years to finally come together. Having started it only to frequently stop working on it numerous times, it is such a relief to finish it!

During the course of writing it, the enemy was very evident in his work against it. Every time that I would begin to work on it again, many times after a long break from writing, I would have a nightmare after going to sleep. Some of the nightmares, were quite severe, not only discouraging me to write this book, but they were the kind of dreams that really test your faith!

I thank God for the endurance he has given me to continue on, and see the work accomplished. If you have a goal and a work to do, keep pushing in and don't give up.　It will all be worth it in the end, just wait and see for yourself. God bless!

# Dream References

## Section 1:
Instances of the word "Dream"

**Genesis 20:3**

But God came to Abimelech in a dream by night, and said to him, Behold, thou art but a dead man, for the woman which thou hast taken; for she is a man's wife.

**Genesis 20:6**

And God said unto him in a dream, Yea, I know that thou didst this in the integrity of thy heart; for I also withheld thee from sinning against me: therefore suffered I thee not to touch her.

**Genesis 31:10**

And it came to pass at the time that the cattle conceived, that I lifted up mine eyes, and saw in a dream, and, behold, the rams which leaped upon the cattle were ringstraked, speckled, and grisled.

## Genesis 31:11

And the angel of God spake unto me in a dream, saying, Jacob: And I said, Here am I.

## Genesis 31:24

And God came to Laban the Syrian in a dream by night, and said unto him, Take heed that thou speak not to Jacob either good or bad.

## Genesis 37:5

And Joseph dreamed a dream, and he told it his brethren: and they hated him yet the more.

## Genesis 37:6

And he said unto them, Hear, I pray you, this dream which I have dreamed:

## Genesis 37:9

And he dreamed yet another dream, and told it his brethren, and said, Behold, I have dreamed a dream more; and, behold, the sun and the moon and the eleven stars made obeisance to me.

## Genesis 37:10

And he told it to his father, and to his brethren: and his father rebuked him, and said unto him, What is this dream that thou hast dreamed? Shall I and thy mother and thy brethren indeed come to bow down ourselves to thee to the earth?

**Genesis 40:5**

And they dreamed a dream both of them, each man his dream in one night, each man according to the interpretation of his dream, the butler and the baker of the king of Egypt, which were bound in the prison.

**Genesis 40:8**

And they said unto him, We have dreamed a dream, and there is no interpreter of it. And Joseph said unto them, Do not interpretations belong to God? tell me them, I pray you.

**Genesis 40:9**

And the chief butler told his dream to Joseph, and said to him, In my dream, behold, a vine was before me;

**Genesis 40:16**

When the chief baker saw that the interpretation was good, he said unto Joseph, I also was in my dream, and, behold, I had three white baskets on my head:

**Genesis 41:7**

And the seven thin ears devoured the seven rank and full ears. And Pharaoh awoke, and, behold, it was a dream.

**Genesis 41:8**

And it came to pass in the morning that his spirit was troubled; and he sent and called for all the magicians of Egypt, and all the wise men thereof: and Pharaoh told them his dream; but there was none that could interpret them unto Pharaoh.

**Genesis 41:11**

And we dreamed a dream in one night, I and he; we dreamed each man according to the interpretation of his dream.

**Genesis 41:12**

And there was there with us a young man, an Hebrew, servant to the captain of the guard; and we told him, and he interpreted to us our dreams; to each man according to his dream he did interpret.

**Genesis 41:15**

And Pharaoh said unto Joseph, I have dreamed a dream, and there is none that can interpret it: and I have heard say of thee, that thou canst understand a dream to interpret it.

**Genesis 41:17**

And Pharaoh said unto Joseph, In my dream, behold, I stood upon the bank of the river:

**Genesis 41:22**

And I saw in my dream, and, behold, seven ears came up in one stalk, full and good:

**Genesis 41:25**

And Joseph said unto Pharaoh, The dream of Pharaoh is one: God hath shewed Pharaoh what he is about to do.

**Genesis 41:26**

The seven good kine are seven years; and the seven good ears are seven years: the dream is one.

## Genesis 41:32

And for that the dream was doubled unto Pharaoh twice; it is because the thing is established by God, and God will shortly bring it to pass.

## Numbers 12:6

And he said, Hear now my words: If there be a prophet among you, I the LORD will make myself known unto him in a vision, and will speak unto him in a dream.

## Judges 7:13

And when Gideon was come, behold, there was a man that told a dream unto his fellow, and said, Behold, I dreamed a dream, and, lo, a cake of barley bread tumbled into the host of Midian, and came unto a tent, and smote it that it fell, and overturned it, that the tent lay along.

## Judges 7:15

And it was so, when Gideon heard the telling of the dream, and the interpretation thereof, that he worshipped, and returned into the host of Israel, and said, Arise; for the LORD hath delivered into your hand the host of Midian.

## 1st Kings 3:5

In Gibeon the LORD appeared to Solomon in a dream by night: and God said, Ask what I shall give thee.

## 1st Kings 3:15

And Solomon awoke; and, behold, it was a dream. And he came to Jerusalem, and stood before the ark of the covenant of the LORD, and offered up burnt offerings, and offered peace offerings, and made a feast to all his servants.

## Job 20:8

He shall fly away as a dream, and shall not be found: yea, he shall be chased away as a vision of the night.

## Job 33:15

In a dream, in a vision of the night, when deep sleep falleth upon men, in slumberings upon the bed;

## Psalms 73:20

As a dream when one awaketh; so, O Lord, when thou awakest, thou shalt despise their image.

## Psalms 126:1

When the LORD turned again the captivity of Zion, we were like them that dream.

## Ecclesiastes 5:3

For a dream cometh through the multitude of business; and a fool's voice is known by multitude of words.

## Isaiah 29:7

And the multitude of all the nations that fight against Ariel, even all that fight against her and her munition, and that distress her, shall be as a dream of a night vision.

## Jeremiah 23:28

The prophet that hath a dream, let him tell a dream; and he that hath my word, let him speak my word faithfully. What is the chaff to the wheat? saith the LORD.

## Daniel 2:3

And the king said unto them, I have dreamed a dream, and my spirit was troubled to know the dream.

## Daniel 2:4

Then spake the Chaldeans to the king in Syriack, O king, live for ever: tell thy servants the dream, and we will shew the interpretation.

## Daniel 2:5

The king answered and said to the Chaldeans, The thing is gone from me: if ye will not make known unto me the dream, with the interpretation thereof, ye shall be cut in pieces, and your houses shall be made a dunghill.

## Daniel 2:6

But if ye shew the dream, and the interpretation thereof, ye shall receive of me gifts and rewards and great honour: therefore shew me the dream, and the interpretation thereof.

## Daniel 2:7

They answered again and said, Let the king tell his servants the dream, and we will shew the interpretation of it.

## Daniel 2:9

But if ye will not make known unto me the dream, there is but one decree for you: for ye have prepared lying and corrupt words to speak before me, till the time be changed: therefore tell me the dream, and I shall know that ye can shew me the interpretation thereof.

**Daniel 2:26**

The king answered and said to Daniel, whose name was Belteshazzar, Art thou able to make known unto me the dream which I have seen, and the interpretation thereof?

**Daniel 2:28**

But there is a God in heaven that revealeth secrets, and maketh known to the king Nebuchadnezzar what shall be in the latter days. Thy dream, and the visions of thy head upon thy bed, are these;

**Daniel 2:36**

This is the dream; and we will tell the interpretation thereof before the king.

**Daniel 2:45**

Forasmuch as thou sawest that the stone was cut out of the mountain without hands, and that it brake in pieces the iron, the brass, the clay, the silver, and the gold; the great God hath made known to the king what shall come to pass hereafter: and the dream is certain, and the interpretation thereof sure.

**Daniel 4:5**

## In The Realm Of Prophetic Dreams

I saw a dream which made me afraid, and the thoughts upon my bed and the visions of my head troubled me.

**Daniel 4:6**

Therefore made I a decree to bring in all the wise men of Babylon before me, that they might make known unto me the interpretation of the dream.

**Daniel 4:7**

Then came in the magicians, the astrologers, the Chaldeans, and the soothsayers: and I told the dream before them; but they did not make known unto me the interpretation thereof.

**Daniel 4:8**

But at the last Daniel came in before me, whose name was Belteshazzar, according to the name of my God, and in whom is the spirit of the holy gods: and before him I told the dream, saying,

**Daniel 4:9**

O Belteshazzar, master of the magicians, because I know that the spirit of the holy gods is in thee, and no secret troubleth thee, tell me the visions of my dream that I have seen, and the interpretation thereof.

**Daniel 4:18**

This dream I king Nebuchadnezzar have seen. Now thou, O Belteshazzar, declare the interpretation thereof, forasmuch as all the wise men of my kingdom are not able to make known unto me the interpretation: but thou art able; for the spirit of the holy gods is in thee.

**Daniel 4:19**

Then Daniel, whose name was Belteshazzar, was astonied for one hour, and his thoughts troubled him. The king spake, and said, Belteshazzar, let not the dream, or the interpretation thereof, trouble thee. Belteshazzar answered and said, My lord, the dream be to them that hate thee, and the interpretation thereof to thine enemies.

## Daniel 7:1

In the first year of Belshazzar king of Babylon Daniel had a dream and visions of his head upon his bed: then he wrote the dream, and told the sum of the matters.

## Joel 2:28

And it shall come to pass afterward, that I will pour out my spirit upon all flesh; and your sons and your daughters shall prophesy, your old men shall dream dreams, your young men shall see visions:

## Matthew 1:20

But while he thought on these things, behold, the angel of the LORD appeared unto him in a dream, saying, Joseph, thou son of David, fear not to take unto thee Mary thy wife: for that which is conceived in her is of the Holy Ghost.

## Matthew 2:12

And being warned of God in a dream that they should not return to Herod, they departed into their own country another way.

## Matthew 2:13

And when they were departed, behold, the angel of the Lord appeareth to Joseph in a dream, saying, Arise, and take the young child and his mother, and flee into Egypt, and be thou there until I bring thee word: for Herod will seek the young child to destroy him.

## Matthew 2:19

But when Herod was dead, behold, an angel of the Lord appeareth in a dream to Joseph in Egypt,

## Matthew 2:22

But when he heard that Archelaus did reign in Judaea in the room of his father Herod, he was afraid to go thither: notwithstanding, being warned of God in a dream, he turned aside into the parts of Galilee:

## Matthew 27:19

When he was set down on the judgment seat, his wife sent unto him, saying, Have thou nothing to do with that just man: for I have suffered many things this day in a dream because of him.

Section 2:

Instances of the word "Dreams"

### Genesis 37:8

And his brethren said to him, Shalt thou indeed reign over us? or shalt thou indeed have dominion over us? And they hated him yet the more for his dreams, and for his words.

### Genesis 37:20

Come now therefore, and let us slay him, and cast him into some pit, and we will say, Some evil beast hath devoured him: and we shall see what will become of his dreams.

### Genesis 41:12

And there was there with us a young man, an Hebrew, servant to the captain of the guard; and we told him, and he interpreted to us our dreams; to each man according to his dream he did interpret.

## Genesis 42:9

And Joseph remembered the dreams which he dreamed of them, and said unto them, Ye are spies; to see the nakedness of the land ye are come.

## Deuteronomy 13:1

If there arise among you a prophet, or a dreamer of dreams, and giveth thee a sign or a wonder,

## Deuteronomy 13:3

Thou shalt not hearken unto the words of that prophet, or that dreamer of dreams: for the LORD your God proveth you, to know whether ye love the LORD your God with all your heart and with all your soul.

## Deuteronomy 13:5

And that prophet, or that dreamer of dreams, shall be put to death; because he hath spoken to turn you away from the LORD your God, which brought you out of the land of Egypt, and redeemed you out of the house of bondage, to thrust thee out of the way which the LORD thy God commanded thee to walk in. So shalt thou put the evil away from the midst of thee.

## 1st Samuel 28:6

And when Saul enquired of the LORD, the LORD answered him not, neither by dreams, nor by Urim, nor by prophets.

**1st Samuel 28:15**

And Samuel said to Saul, Why hast thou disquieted me, to bring me up? And Saul answered, I am sore distressed; for the Philistines make war against me, and God is departed from me, and answereth me no more, neither by prophets, nor by dreams: therefore I have called thee, that thou mayest make known unto me what I shall do.

**Job 7:14**

Then thou scarest me with dreams, and terrifiest me through visions:

**Ecclesiastes 5:7**

For in the multitude of dreams and many words there are also divers vanities: but fear thou God.

**Jeremiah 23:27**

Which think to cause my people to forget my name by their dreams which they tell every man to his neighbour, as their fathers have forgotten my name for Baal.

**Jeremiah 23:32**

Behold, I am against them that prophesy false dreams, saith the LORD, and do tell them, and cause my people to err by their lies, and by their lightness; yet I sent them not, nor commanded them: therefore they shall not profit this people at all, saith the LORD.

**Jeremiah 29:8**

For thus saith the LORD of hosts, the God of Israel; Let not your prophets and your diviners, that be in the midst of you, deceive you, neither hearken to your dreams which ye cause to be dreamed.

**Daniel 1:17**

As for these four children, God gave them knowledge and skill in all learning and wisdom: and Daniel had understanding in all visions and dreams.

**Daniel 2:1**

And in the second year of the reign of Nebuchadnezzar Nebuchadnezzar dreamed dreams, wherewith his spirit was troubled, and his sleep brake from him.

**Daniel 2:2**

Then the king commanded to call the magicians, and the astrologers, and the sorcerers, and the Chaldeans, for to shew the king his dreams. So they came and stood before the king.

## Daniel 5:12

Forasmuch as an excellent spirit, and knowledge, and understanding, interpreting of dreams, and shewing of hard sentences, and dissolving of doubts, were found in the same Daniel, whom the king named Belteshazzar: now let Daniel be called, and he will shew the interpretation.

## Joel 2:28

And it shall come to pass afterward, that I will pour out my spirit upon all flesh; and your sons and your daughters shall prophesy, your old men shall dream dreams, your young men shall see visions:

## Zechariah 10:2

For the idols have spoken vanity, and the diviners have seen a lie, and have told false dreams; they comfort in vain: therefore they went their way as a flock, they were troubled, because there was no shepherd.

Woodrow Polston

In The Realm Of Prophetic Dreams

## Also From Polston House

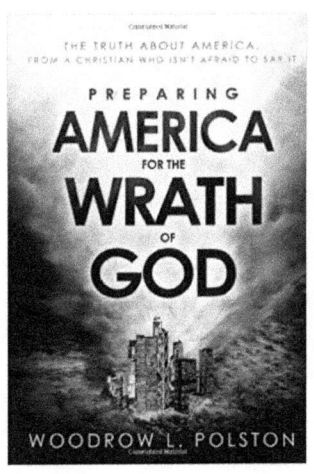

Wars and rumors of wars. Deadly hurricanes, tornadoes, and earthquakes. Intense political, economic, and social unrest around the world. Signs that we are living in the end times are all around us. The day is quickly approaching when we will pay the price for the sins that connect America from coast to coast. It is time for sinners and Christians alike to stop pretending that the sins of our nation will go unpunished. In *Preparing America for the Wrath of God,* author Woodrow Polston unveils shocking biblical prophecy and revelation, calling America to repent and turn from her sins before it is too late.

Woodrow Polston

*Preparing America for the Wrath of God* will inspire you to devote yourself fully to Christ and boldly share His life-changing message with everyone you meet.

In The Realm Of Prophetic Dreams

# Also From Polston House

Who is he that was spoken of old, destined to be the final ruler before the return of Christ? What will the world look like under his reign? Is it possible that he is alive today, walking among us unknown until he receives his power and authority? In Enemy of the Saints, Woodrow Polston reveals key characteristics of the man who will become the Antichrist, as well as those who will follow him. Enemy of the Saints exposes the rise of Christian persecution and the increased division within the church. The rapid decline of moral values and much evidence that proves just how late the hour is in which we live. Enemy of the Saints will empower you to walk in bold faith, despite the opposition that lies ahead. With prophetic insight regarding the enemy, you will be better equipped to discern who he is and the motives of those who will blindly follow him.

## Also From Polston House

The enemy of our souls wants your company for the rest of eternity in Hell! While Satan has many different approaches, one of the most subtle and cunning, is through his ministers. These people go forth not into the world, but into the church. Is there any better place to hide than right out in the open disguised as everyone else? Lighthearted sentiments, promises of worldly prosperity and eloquent lies are their bait, and you are the prey. In False Hope and the Prophets of Doom, Author Miryah Polston exposes many of the devil's tricks and guises. Stop having your itching ears tickled and move forward into the true light of Christ!

Woodrow Polston

In The Realm Of Prophetic Dreams

## Also From Polston House

Enoch, the seventh from Adam, one of only two men to be taken up by God. His time spent on earth was just prior to the flood, when the Sons of God were corrupting humanity. His book, quoted in the New Testament, reveals much insight today. In Unlocking the Book of Enoch, we will discover the origin of demons, witchcraft, warfare, and much more. Were the events of the Bible revealed in his visions? Did he prophesy of Jesus, the tribulation and the great judgment? Does it line up with scripture? His prophecy begins with the statement, "This is for a remote generation." Are we that generation?

Woodrow Polston

## Also From Polston House

"Thomana did not look back. He knew that if he did that he would not go. He would stay and die with the woman he loved. But he could not give the baby over to this fate. He had promised." Song doesn't know her dad's terrifying secret, and if she did her simple world would come crashing down. Leigh is a simple woman leading a good life, but if her real past was revealed it just might kill her. When these two women are thrown together everything they thought was real is shaken. Can they work with each other to survive, or will the one who has been searching for them achieve his hideous goal?

Woodrow Polston

## Also From Polston House

What happens in the backwoods of southern Missouri.... Don't always stay in them there backwoods. When an old moonshiner catches his own kinfolk sneaking around his still, does he shoot em? Will anyone believe Tuffy and Doc really seen Bigfoot while picking berries in the woods? Do the ghosts of the past still haunt the hills and the hollers? Get settled up next to a fire and find out, in the Legends of Leeper Holler.

Woodrow Polston

## Also From Polston House

"Everything that contained microchips has been rendered useless. Including all transportation, save that of the government. According to local government, the President has announced that we have come under attack by an unknown foreign enemy. As the majority of the country was instantly powered down, millions of workers and business owners across the nation poured out of their dark buildings and into the streets. Society was in a state of confusion, many did not know the magnitude of what had happened. And everyone was idle in expectation of the power coming back on. When nightfall came, and darkness covered the cities, a lot of people began to act like animals."

In The Realm Of Prophetic Dreams

# Also From Polston House

Woodrow Polston

## About Polston House Publishing

Polston House Publishing was Founded in 2016 by Woodrow and Miryah Polston. After acquiring rights to numerous titles from various imprints, the faith based family business was born. With the intention of publishing Christian and family friendly literature, the number of Authors and works continue to grow. Visit the official website at Polstonhouse.com for more information.

Woodrow Polston

In The Realm Of Prophetic Dreams

## Also From Polston House

## Coming soon

Woodrow Polston

In The Realm Of Prophetic Dreams

Woodrow Polston

www.ingramcontent.com/pod-product-compliance
Lightning Source LLC
Chambersburg PA
CBHW061332040426
42444CB00011B/2880